Old KIRKCUDBRIGH

by
Alastair Penman

CW00349684

St Mary Street.

© Alastair Penman 1998
First published in the United Kingdom, 1998,
by Stenlake Publishing, Ochiltree Sawmill, The Lade,
Ochiltree, Ayrshire, KA18 2NX
Telephone / Fax: 01290 423114

ISBN 1 84033 037 6

THE PUBLISHERS REGRET THAT THEY CANNOT SUPPLY
COPIES OF ANY PICTURES FEATURED IN THIS BOOK.

ACKNOWLEDGEMENTS

E.J. Cochrane, Daphne Brooke, Ian Devlin, Jeanette Millar and Jo Laurie.
Special thanks to Dr David Devereux, Curator of the Stewartry Museum,
Kirkcudbright, for all his encouragement and help in researching this book.

Looking along Oakley Avenue towards the entrance to St Mary's Isle, a house built on the site of the Priory of Santa Maria de Traill. Plague regulations were applied to travellers to the priory in 1578, 1599, 1644 and 1648. In 1599 travel was forbidden beyond Urr, and no gypsies or vagrants were allowed to enter the burgh of Kirkcudbright because the 'pest' or pestilence was in Dumfries. The town gates were often guarded by burgesses during such emergencies to ensure that undesirables such as wandering beggars didn't gain entry.

INTRODUCTION

Few towns in Britain can rival Kirkcudbright's varied history. There is plentiful evidence of prehistoric activity, with cup-and-ring marked rocks, Bronze Age burial mounds and Iron Age hill forts in the vicinity. If, as is thought to be the case, the Romans used the port at Kirkcudbright – as they did across the River Nith at Caerlaverock – there is also a very early seagoing connection.

The burgh stands on a gravel ridge, approximately along the line of High Street, and was originally surrounded by creeks beyond which were swamplands and the tidal estuary of the River Dee. A burn which flowed into the river rose in the vicinity of the present day car park in Harbour Square, and would have taken its course across St Cuthbert Street, through the row of shops and houses and on up to Castle Street. These features meant that the settlement could be easily defended; when the tide was high, it was virtually an island.

The name Kirkcudbright is derived from Anglo-Saxon and Gaelic and translates as 'the church of St Cuthbert'. It probably dates from the seventh century foundation of a church dedicated to Cuthbert on the hill overlooking the burgh. In 875, when Norsemen raided the coast of Northumbria the monks on Lindisfarne were forced to flee, bringing with them their holy relics including the bones of St Cuthbert and the head of St Oswald, King of Northumbria. One of their sanctuaries was Kirkcudbright. In 1164 the town is referred to as *Cuthbrictischirche*, and described as being 'situated in Galloway and . . . made charming by a sweet river flowing through its suburbs'.

Roland, Lord of Galloway from 1185 to 1200, had a residence in Kirkcudbright, and a charter from the reign of King William 'The Lion' (1165-1214) granted the priory on St Mary's Isle 'one-tenth of the provisions of the said Roland's house in food and drink, wax and tallow and everything else pertaining to his table in Kirkcudbright'.

Between 1200 and 1230 a group of Kirkcudbright merchants, who sailed between the town and Dublin, can be identified through the Dublin City Rolls. There seems to have been a burgh with a provost *c.*1220-1230, and it is known that James II elevated the burgh to Royal status, or at least confirmed that status, in 1455, after the fall of the House of Douglas. The burghers of Kirkcudbright had furnished the royal army with assistance in the form of iron bars or 'gauds' which were used to build a monster bombard or cannon. According to tradition this was used to batter down the walls of Threave Castle, the Douglas's stronghold further up the River Dee. Some sources say the big gun was none other than 'Mons Meg' which now stands on display in Edinburgh Castle.

The fortification Castledykes was built during the reign of Alexander III, and in 1300 was given over to the English King Edward I during his 'invasion' of Galloway. Kirkcudbright's harbour was used by the English army, who shipped supplies across the Solway into it. During the Bruce-Balliol wars, which some people refer to as the Wars of Scottish Independence, the castle was occupied firstly by the English and then by the Bruce's themselves. After Edward Bruce became Lord of Galloway in 1307, his forces were garrisoned at Castledykes and kept order in the name of his royal brother, Robert. By 1330-1331 the port's customs duties were being recorded in the Scottish Royal Exchequer Rolls. Salted salmon was almost a currency in the town at a later recording.

One must assume that in order to feed the community of Kirkcudbright there were open fields and communal parks immediately outside the burgh boundary. After the death of Bruce, Scottish politics became somewhat involved and it all ended up with Edward Balliol being proclaimed King – albeit a puppet of English masters – until 1356. Kirkcudbright town lands were wasted and yielded little in the way of harvest at this time. The result was famine. This was followed by the dark era of Douglas rule in Galloway, during which the Tutor of Bombie, Sir Patrick MacLellan, was murdered in Threave Castle.

Kirkcudbright has been the victim of attack on various occasions. Manxmen destroyed the town in 1507, and it was attacked by the English raider Carleton in 1547, although he couldn't get through the defences and was forced to retreat the way he had come. After the Battle of Pinkie, in the early years of the rule of Mary, Queen of Scots, the town was besieged and, again, withstood the invader. The good burghers 'barr'd their gates and kept their dikes, for the town is diked on both sides, with a gate at the water-ward and a gate in the cross-end of the fell-ward' (the latter gate was known as the Meikle Yett).

King William III embarked his troops for the invasion of Ireland from Kirkcudbright, and the town played a role during the 'Killing Times' – that era of stound and sair disgrace when the Presbyterian Covenanters were hounded, in some cases to their deaths, by the king's military persecutors. The Tolbooth was attacked and Covenanter prisoners set free. Silent testimony to their cause can still be found today, in the kirkyard up on the hill, where three of 'the martyrs of the Covenant' lie buried.

Kirkcudbright has successfully survived these vicissitudes. It has been burned and harried by foreign foes, harried and bullied by domestic ones, but has risen above all of this and emerged into the present, proud of its often turbulent past.

THE LAKE ROAD, KIRKCUDBRIGHT

Copyright
Kbt. 38

Manxman's Lake, on the eastern shore of Kirkcudbright Bay, probably takes its name from the days of the piratical forays of the Manxmen. In 1507 the Earl of Derby, at the head of a large force of Manxmen, attacked Kirkcudbright and burned most of the town to the ground. Records state that the raid was so destructive that many of the houses remained unoccupied and in ruins for several years afterwards. On a clear day the Isle of Man can be seen from this point. The gentleman in the picture is one of the Picken family from nearby Torrs Farm, noted breeders of Clydesdale horses.

OLD DOVECOTE AND GRANARY, CANNEE, KIRKCUDBRIGHT

Cannee Farm has been described as an informally grouped mid-nineteenth century steading with crow-stepped gable ranges, some of which have now been converted into housing. The round windmill-like tower, actually a granary, was constructed in four stages, each of which was marked off with a rat course, a projecting ledge designed to make it more difficult for vermin to climb up the walls and into the building. The granary was subsequently used as a doocot, and is one of few to survive in Galloway.

During the First World War munitions were manufactured at the Tongland Works. In the twenties, the Galloway Engineering Company, a subsidiary of Arrol-Johnston and one of the three 'big A's' of the pioneering days of Scottish motoring (the others being Albion and Argyll) took over the works. They built the Galloway two-seater car there. It had a 10.5 hp engine, Zenith carburettor and 8' 6" wheelbase. Initially only one model was made, costing £550, but in 1924 four models were on display at the Scottish Motor Show, a two-seater (£265), four-seater (£298) and two Galloway coupés (£350 including double dickey seat). There was no choice of colours; the two- and four-seaters were brown and the coupés blue. In 1925 increased demand allowed Arrol-Johnston to reduce their prices, but the works closed down c.1926, although production continued in Dumfries. Arrol-Johnston merged with the Aster Engineering Company in London, but the new company went into liquidation in 1930. The Tongland Works employed more Kirkcudbright people than any other concern in the area.

Silk Factory, Kirkcudbright.

During the early years of the Second World War Kirkcudbright's silk factory (formerly the premises of the Galloway Engineering Company) produced parachutes for the Royal Air Force. Employees came from all over the area to work there, and it was not uncommon for women and girls from as far afield as Castle Douglas to cycle or walk the nine miles to and from work every day. Just over the river from this site are the remains of Tongland Abbey. Its main claim to fame was that one of its abbots was the earliest pioneer of aviation in Scotland. Father John Damian, an alchemist and favourite of King James IV, was ridiculed by the Scots poet Dunbar in a scathing satire called *The Frenzeit Frier of Tungland*. The abbot claimed, before the king, that he would fly from the battlements of Stirling Castle to Paris in a fraction of the time it would take a messenger to get there on horseback. They set off at the same time, and while the messenger reached Paris, Damian fell into a dung heap at the bottom of the castle walls and broke his thigh. He blamed the failure of his aircraft on the fact that he had constructed his 'wings' from the feathers of common birds as opposed to those of the more exotic species.

John Houston was postman for the rural area between Kirkcudbright and Borgue at the end of the nineteenth and beginning of the twentieth centuries. Famous as the 'Kirkcudbright weather prophet', he made forecasts which he displayed on the board behind him. His observations were taken from the sky alone. According to him its appearance described the wind, and the wind ruled the weather, with the lower sky indicating prevailing conditions and the upper sky revealing future changes. With close observation and careful calculation John found that he could arrive at a very accurate weather forecast. This picture shows him with his 'official' issue post office pony and trap *c*.1900.

Kirkcudbright Station was opened in 1864, and the line that it served carried passengers and goods from the royal burgh to Dumfries via Castle Douglas for just over a hundred years. It experienced its blackest day in 1962, when an engine collided with some coaches standing at the platform. They in turn crashed through the buffers, carrying them away, running straight through the station wall and coming to rest in the street, having almost entered Mr Patterson's ice-cream parlour. In 1967 the town council purchased the entire site from British Railways and built houses on most of it. The only surviving part of the complex is the old ticket office and station-master's quarters, which were turned into The Ingle restaurant.

JohnstoneSchool.Kirkcudbright.

A local merchant, William Johnston, bequeathed the sum of £5,000 for the building of the Johnston School in 1848. Tuition was free for poor children, and at a time when most schools made a charge for their services it provided innovative access to education for many working class families. The sum of £2,000 was used to buy land and provide the school building and the remaining £3,000 was invested to pay for the running costs and the dominies' salaries. Unfortunately Mr Johnston did not live to see his project completed. In 1933 the school was extensively rebuilt, but the tower and wall of the original building have survived.

Townend and Barhill. The Selkirk Arms Hotel, on the left, is famous for its connections with Robert Burns, who was said to have stayed there in 1794. The end of this street was originally called 'the fontainblue' after the drinking trough for horses which stood behind the Selkirk Arms. The local children, or 'inborn bairns', used this name before it was called Townend. Before St Mary Street was laid out in the early nineteenth century this was the old road to Dumfries.

The whole of the Barhill area has now been built upon. It was near here that royalist troops, sent into the area during the agrarian disturbances of the early 1720s, were barracked. Bands of discontented small tenant farmers, the Levellers as they were called, rose in open rebellion at the enclosure of agricultural land which was turned into vast cattle parks by unscrupulous and wealthy landowners. They burnt the new fences and overturned recently built dry-stane dykes, causing much grief to the local landowners until eventually the military had to be called in. By April 1724 the Levellers were so well organised that a further six troops of dragoons were rushed from Edinburgh and billeted in Kirkcudbright. In June the rising was crushed by sheer force of numbers. Some of the ringleaders, including, as local legend has it, the self-styled 'King of The Gypsies', Billy Marshall, were lodged in the Tolbooth. Prosecutions and heavy fines followed, but the vast amount of local sympathy for the plight of the Levellers, including support from the pulpits, seems to have done much to reduce the severity of the law enforcement agencies.

High Millburn Street, Kirkcudbright.

Millburn Street got its name from the Mill Burn, so called after a corn mill which was built on the site of an earlier fulling mill. The road was formerly called 'The King's High Way' and originally led to Tongland and Dumfries. Mill-Burn was once a separate settlement outside the burgh boundary of Kirkcudbright 'at some small distance . . . indeed almost joining it, at right angles', as Robert Heron described it in 1792. In 1598 the bailies and burgesses of Dumfries raided Kirkcudbright in retaliation for what they considered the injustice of some of their customs duties on ships' cargoes being 'stolen' by the port of Kirkcudbright. They intended to surprise and sack the town, but were driven off by the townspeople behind their secure defences. Instead they set fire to Millburn and burnt down some barns, for which damage they were later forced to make reparation.

Millburn Street. In 1491, under the Great Seal of Scotland, King James IV confirmed a charter giving power to Thomas MacLellan of Bombie to construct an aqueduct and a croft commonly called Clark Hill, along with another croft called Crooked Acre on the common lands of the burgh on the west and the lands of Lochfergus on the north. The annual rent was to be 40 shillings (i.e. 3 merks) and all the burgesses of Kirkcudbright were to have their wool 'teased and sheared and woollen cloth dressed at half the price received from others'. Janet McRobert of Milnburn was arraigned before Kirkcudbright Kirk Session in 1701, charged with making cows ill, dogs mad, and with having the Devil appear in her house on regular occasions. Accused of the crime of witchcraft she was banished to Ireland. Only three years prior to this, another witch, Elspeth McEwen, was strangled to death and her corpse then burned.

A document of 1491, bearing the seal of King James IV, granted permission for the building of a fulling mill in Millburn Street (above). When visiting the town the king confirmed a charter originally drawn up by 'the Provost, Bailies and Community of the Burgh of Kirkcudbright conveying to Thomas MacLellan of Bombie in feu farm the liberty of the burn, known as the Kirk Burn, where it flows into the River Dee, with power to build a Fulling Mill and a House on the said burn wherever seems best'. In the latter half of the nineteenth century there was a tannery, snuff mill and bleach fields for the laying out of treated cloth near this spot.

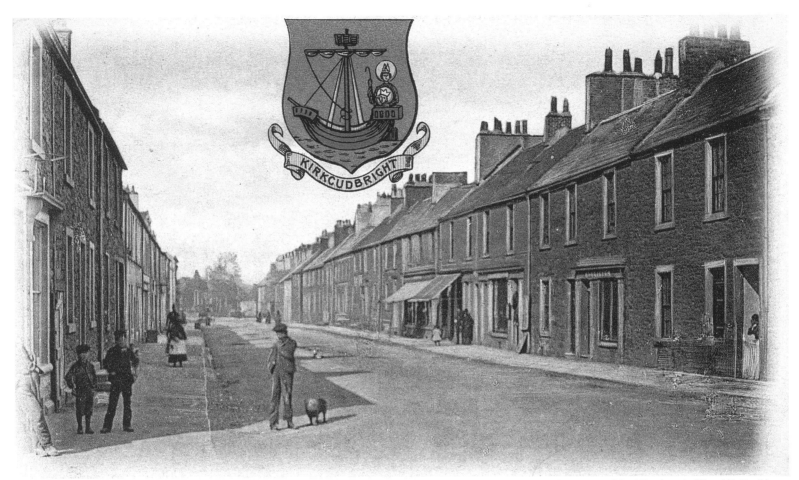

Castle Street looking towards Greyfriars Church. One of the earliest references to Kirkcudbright is found in Reginald of Durham's life of St Cuthbert, the saint who features prominently on the burgh coat of arms. His presence denotes Ailred of Rievaulx's visit to the town on the feast of St Cuthbert on 20 March 1165, when some rather pagan customs were being practised at the old kirk up on the hill, overlooking the town. It is said that some clerics were bating a bull which they had tied to a tree, and intended to offer as an oblation. When ordered to desist by Ailred, one of them told him to mind his own business, and also spoke disrespectfully of St Cuthbert. No sooner had the insult been uttered than the bull escaped and gored some of its torturers, badly injuring the ringleader who had insulted Ailred – much to his delight, we are told. He interpreted the incident as a triumph of Christianity over Paganism in Kirkcudbright.

In 1684 the town of Kirkcudbright was paying a man a small coin and a pint of ale a day for 'throwing down stones from Dundrennan Abbey'. On an early map the former abbey is marked as a quarry, and legend has it that some of those stones were subsequently incorporated into the Tolbooth. 'Jougs' – iron collars used for securing wrongdoers by the neck – still hang beside the door of the Tolbooth tower. These were originally fastened to a wooden post set up at the tron, or weighing beam. A malefactor would be clamped into the irons and made to stand for a certain length of time or at a particular time on certain days, e.g. market days, as a humiliating punishment. Many of the crimes for which people were punished were breaches of church discipline, sabbath-breaking for instance. The sentences were passed by the burgh court which had malefactors passed on to it for sentencing by the notorious kirk session.

The King's Arms Inn, on the left, was conveniently situated adjacent to the Tolbooth, once the centre of burgh affairs. As the principal inn of the town it was commonly called the Heid Inn, being a popular place to stay and a suitable venue for official functions or meetings. When the County Commissioners held their meetings in the Tolbooth – usually two-day affairs – most of the delegates stayed in the King's Arms where, it was said, a special wine cellar was kept solely for their enjoyment as they were known to be gentlemen of refined tastes. Samuel Malcolmson is recorded as being its owner in 1789; another member of the family, Robert Malcolmson, corresponded regularly with Sir Walter Scott and supplied him with tales of the area which Scott used in his novels. Earlier this century the property was purchased by William Robson, well-known as one of a group of local artists. When workmen were stripping off old wallpaper in one of the rooms, they found a piece of writing on the wall bearing the signature of one R. Burns! The smuggler John McClure, who had a path running from his garden right down to the River Dee, lived at 56 High Street.

Looking up High Street towards the Tolbooth. The building on the right was demolished to make way for modern police houses, much to the detriment of this part of the street. This is probably one of the oldest parts of the town, and it was near here, at Castledykes, that King Edward I spent time with his queen and court during 1300. In 1455 James II stayed in the burgh while his army gathered at Causewayend to smash the power of the Douglas family, ensconced behind the thick walls of Threave Castle. King Henry VI fled here with his Queen and court after his defeat at Towton in 1461. He remained in the burgh while his wife went to Edinburgh to visit the Scottish Queen: 'the Kyng Harry is at Kirkcowbry with 4 men and a childe'. He returned to England in disguise in 1463. In 1508 King James IV visited the town 'when he was entertained with all the hospitality of the age when show took the place of opulence'.

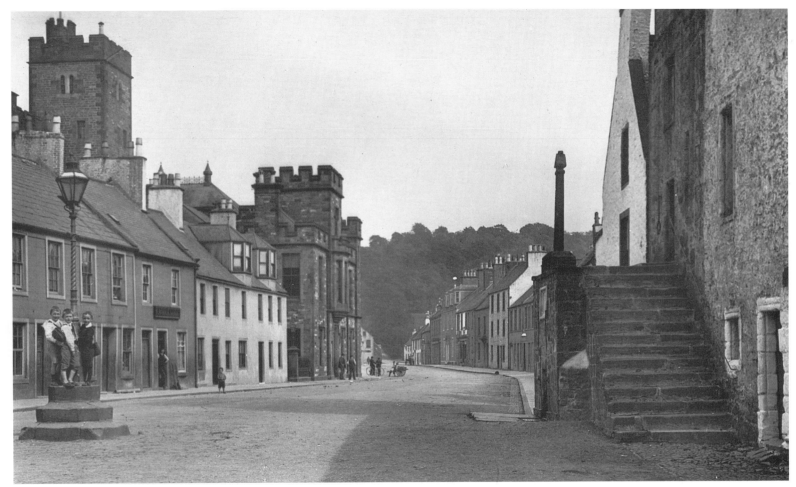

The castellated tower of the former town gaol is on the left. The Mercat Cross, at the top of the stairs leading up to the Tolbooth tower, bears the date 1610. It once stood on the pedestal to the left where the three youngsters are standing, but was moved to the Tolbooth for safety. It is hardly surprising that a decision was made to relocate this ancient symbol of urban power; it was at this spot that the wassail-bowl was wont to be filled on festive occasions. One of the water cisterns introduced into the town in 1763 is under the steps. On the front is a tablet bearing the inscription:

This fount, not riches, life supplies,
Art gives what Nature here denies.
Posterity must surely bless
St Cuthbert's sons who purchased this.
Water introduced 23rd of March, 1763.

High Street again with the Selkirk Arms, a hotel since 1777, on the right. In 1845 it is recorded that there were twenty-seven inns or houses licensed to sell spiritous liquors in the Parish of Kirkcudbright. The same source states that much coal and lime came in to the town from Cumberland, and a great many articles of 'general traffic', such as flour, herrings, groceries, haberdasheries, hardware, iron, slates, freestone, etc., were conveyed from Liverpool and other places by land and sea. A socket stone marking the position of one of the pillars of the 'Meikle Yett' or town gate, lies in the roadway just beyond the hotel. It was on these gates that the severed heads of criminals, rebels and traitors were displayed on poles set up for the purpose. In troubled times the burghers had to give 'watch and ward' services; in return they were granted feus on nominal terms.

An early photograph of the Tolbooth when it had a square clock face. This clock, which only had one hand, is now in the Stewartry Museum. It was moved off-centre because in its original position people couldn't see it from the bottom of the street; the view was blocked by the chimneys of the houses in front of it. The Tolbooth was the town gaol; not just where offenders were imprisoned but also where they were punished. As was the practice in other Scottish burghs in the seventeenth century, criminals could be branded on the cheek, hand or shoulder for offences such as theft. Punishment might also involve being tied to a post and flogged – 'scourgit' – and then being banished from the town, sometimes for life.

A variety of sadistic tortures were used on those accused of witchcraft or treason. Racks and pulleys, 'the pilliewinkies' or thumbscrews, introduced into Scotland from Russia by General 'Tam' Dalyell in the seventeenth century, pincers (both hot and cold), deprivation of sleep and 'examination' by prodding, were among the punishments meted out. One of the Tolbooth's most famous inmates was the witch Elspeth McEwen. She was systematically tortured to make her admit to the crime of witchcraft, and after two years of terrible treatment confessed all and begged for death. Found guilty of 'a compact and correspondence with the Devil, and of charms and of accession to malefices' her body was burnt after she had been strangled – a common end for a witch in Scotland – 'worried at ane stake till they be deid and thairafter their bodies to be burnt to ashes'. The execution was very unpopular and the executioner had to be kept in the Tolbooth for his own safety. Elspeth's crime was that she had made her neighbour's hens stop laying and that she had kept a moveable pin (her 'kipple-fit pin') with which she drew off milk from their cows at will.

The 'condemned cell', so graphically described in *Guy Mannering* by Sir Walter Scott, is in the Tolbooth. It was there that two Covenanters, William Hunter and Robert Smith, spent their final hours before being executed by John Graham of Claverhouse, the 'Bonnie Dundee' of legend and history. They had been involved in a raid on the Tolbooth, on 16 December 1684, when a band of a hundred Covenanters attacked the gaol, threw open the cells and released all the prisoners. During the raid a prison guard was killed. Claverhouse and his dragoons pursued the Covenanters and, after a skirmish with them at Bridge of Dee where he was nearly killed, finally ran some of them to ground on Auchencloy Moor in Girthon Parish. The Covenanters' ringleader James McMichael was killed, and Smith and Hunter were captured and brought back to Kirkcudbright in chains. Claverhouse had been appointed Bailie of the Regality of Tongland in 1682, and in that capacity he presided over a court which sentenced them both to be hanged. They are buried in St Cuthbert's kirkyard overlooking the town.

A view of the Tolbooth when its walls were harled. The central section of the building, originally a house, is the oldest, having been built between 1625 and 1629. The tower was added in 1644. It burnt down and the join in the masonry where the rebuilding took place can still be clearly seen. The windowless section on the right was added in the 1750s. Part of the Tolbooth housed the armoury and drill-room of the 1st Kirkcudbright Rifle Volunteers. The weather-vane surmounting the spire represents a full-rigged three-master ship of the seventeenth century, pointing to the town's long association with the sea. There was a small dairy to the left of where the horse and cart are.

St Mary Street with the town hall, opened in 1879, on the right. The Stewartry Museum once occupied the top floor, but has now moved along the street to its own magnificent building. In the distance is the spire of St Mary's Church. St Cuthbert's Church lies in behind the trees on the left.

St. Mary Street, Kirkcudbright.

St Mary's Church has now been converted into a block of flats. The horse and cart on the right is that of the railway station delivery service and the gentleman to the right of it the delivery man. In the heyday of the railway a delivery service made calls around the burgh several times a day.

St Cuthbert Street looking towards MacLellan's Castle, with carriages belonging to guests parked in front of the Royal Hotel. The horses were taken up neighbouring Mews Lane by the hotel's ostler and stabled for the duration of their owners' visit. According to some local sources, the Lords of Kirkcudbright, who had once lived in splendour in the castle, were so reduced in circumstances by the eighteenth century that they were forced to live in a small thatched cottage situated nearly opposite the present County Buildings in High Street. In the early part of the century, Lord Kirkcudbright kept an ale house across from the castle where, on Fridays, he hobnobbed with the local farmers and country-folk who came to market. His son, Lord John, greased the guest's boots, and Lady Betty, his daughter, made the beds. Beyond the hotel, on the left, is the memorial to the Earl of Selkirk, erected in 1885.

St. Cuthbert Street, Kirkcudbright

When MacLellan's Castle (background) was built, it had a wide prospect all round, with views overlooking the river and the orchards and gardens of the Friary, founded for Franciscans, or Gray Friars, during the reign of King Alexander II. In the reign of David II one of the friars, John Carpenter, was distinguished for his talents as an engineer and for his dexterity in contriving instruments of war. He fortified Dumbarton Castle for which he was awarded a pension of £20 sterling a year. When this photograph was taken more of the properties in St Cuthbert Street were private houses and fewer were shops than is the case now.

St Cuthbert Street and Harbour Square with the Steam Packet Inn, centre, and an early caravan, a harbinger of those that bring so many welcome visitors to the town now. This particular one belonged to a travelling preacher who made regular visits to the burgh. The former harbour dock was situated near where the caravan is parked. Built in the late eighteenth century, it consisted of a timber platform laid on a high sandbank, accompanied by a boatbuilding yard. It was removed when the new harbour was constructed c.1910.

St Cuthbert Street. In 1845 it was recorded that 'formerly Kirkcudbright was celebrated for its manufacture of gloves, and more recently, of boots and shoes . . . There were, at one time, though on a small scale, manufacturies of soap, candles, and leather; and kelp was also frequently made upon the shores. On the ground occupied by The Academy, once stood a brewery: and a house yet remains that was built for a snuff mill.'

The County Buildings and Tolbooth before much of the land in the foreground was built on. The photograph was taken by a Mr McConchie. In 1455 King James II conferred royal burgh status on Kirkcudbright. This was to reward the MacLellan family, then provosts, for their role in the defeat of the Douglas's during the king's siege of Threave Castle, the last Douglas stronghold in the south to hold out. As a contemporary poem tells us:

Each burgher of St Cuthbert town,
Weigh'd by the Douglas bondage down,
Brought to the leaguer of the Crown
The tribute of his iron store.

The iron was use to build the monster cannon, 'Mons Meg', which battered the castle into submission.

The view from the top of County Buildings with MacLellan's Castle and the iron bridge over the Dee estuary to the left. From left to right, the spires are those of St Mary's, the United Free and St Cuthbert's Churches. The street running from the centre of the photograph to the bottom right hand corner is Castle Street. Robert Heron, writing in 1792, described the burgh as consisting of 'one long, bending street, extending backward from the river side. The houses are, for the greater part, of decent structure, consisting commonly of two storeys, and having their roofs slated. Several closes, or narrow cross streets extend backwards, on both sides . . . The Dee is crossed in a Ferry-Boat.'

In 1792 Robert Heron wrote that: 'the harbour furnishes dilse, tangle and common seaweed. A considerable quantity of the latter is cut, made into kelp, and sold for the soap and bottle manufactures'. The port was once a busy place, the Custom House there having a comptroller, surveyor, landwaiter, four tidemen and four boatmen. In 1792 there were 28 vessels of 1,058 tons registered at the port, and in 1801 37 vessels of 1,648 tons. There were two well-equipped shipbuilding yards in the burgh.

The Dee Bridge was opened on 8 July 1868 to a salvo of three guns fired by members of the Kirkcudbright Artillery, and several shots from the deck gun of the steamer *Countess of Galloway*. It originally consisted of five fixed spans and a sixth longer span which turned on a large cast-iron cylinder filled with concrete. The swinging apparatus allowed the passage of ships to Tongland, and could easily be operated by one man. Two plaques bearing the names of the contractors, Messrs Hopkins, Gilkes & Co., Middlesborough, are now fastened to the railings in front of the Stewartry Museum. The cost of building the bridge was £10,000, about half of which was raised by public subscription, the other half coming from the Road Trustees.

RIVER AND HARBOUR, KIRKCUDBRIGHT

During the seventeenth century little trade passed through Kirkcudbright's port. Thomas Tucker, the Cromwellian Commissioner, described it as 'one of the best ports on this side of Scotland' but added that there were 'few, and these very poore, merchants, or pedlars rather, tradeing with Ireland'. A little later, in 1724, Daniel Defoe of *Robinson Crusoe* fame commented that 'Kirkcubry is a harbour without ships, a port without trade, a fishery without nets, a people without business; and which is worse than all, they do not seem to desire business, much less do they understand it . . . there is not a vessel, that deserves the name of a ship, belongs to it'. The construction of a new harbour, *c.*1911, led to an increase in trade and prosperity within the burgh.

NEW HARBOUR, KIRKCUDBRIGHT

When this photograph was taken *c.*1920, goods and commodities arrived in Kirkcudbright from such places as Liverpool, Dublin, the Isle of Man and Glasgow. There was once a brisk trade in wine. It is recorded that, in 1511, a tun of wine was bought at Kirkcudbright and sent to Sir John Musgray. The cost of the wine was £8 and the carriage of it by boat was 56 shillings. An entry in the English State Papers for the year 1523 describes the contents of 'five more ships' that visited the port, four of which were laden with flour and wine, and two with cannons and powder. The fifth vessel was a French privateer carrying 'victuals for sale'.

The Harbour, Kirkcudbright

Valentine's Series

This picture shows the old harbour, which was filled in in 1911. The ships *Daisy* and *Utopia* regularly plied their trade in and out of the port of Kirkcudbright. During the course of the First World War not a single vessel appeared in the harbour, and it was not until a year after the end of hostilities that the first steamer arrived, the harbinger of more prosperous times. In 1845 'two commodious steam-boats' sailed regularly from Kirkcudbright to Liverpool, once a week in the summer and once a fortnight in winter. Trade with the small seaports along the coast declined with the building of the railways, and the branch line to Kirkcudbright ultimately destroyed the viability of the port.

Harbour Cottage Art Gallery stands between MacLellan's Castle and the granary (right), now converted into flats. Legend has it that it was from Kirkcudbright that William Wallace set sail for France after the disaster at Falkirk, in 1298, having resigned his post as guardian of Scotland. He was said to have been accompanied by one of the MacLellan's of Bombie and 50 loyal followers. The steamer in the centre of the picture is a cargo ship, *The Countess of Galloway*, not to be confused with the famous nineteenth century steam packet ship of the same name. She steamed round the coastline carrying both cargo and passengers to other local ports such as the Isle of Whithorn and Garlieston.

Following a petition signed by 398 people 'interested in the navigation of the Solway Firth', work on the Little Ross lighthouse began in 1841. The light was first operated on 1 January 1843. It was designed by Alan Stevenson, uncle of the novelist Robert Louis Stevenson, and although it incorporated a dioptric light with a new system of metallic mirrors above and below the lenses, Stevenson did not regard his design as a success. Little Ross was the scene of a particularly gruesome event in the 1960s when an assistant keeper robbed and murdered the occasional light-keeper and fled. He was eventually captured and sentenced to death at the High Court in Dumfries, although the sentence was later commuted to life imprisonment. The lighthouse is still in operation, guarding the narrow seas outside the port of Kirkcudbright – the bay and adjoining waters of which once swarmed with 'Pyrates' such as Captain Leonard Robertson, burgess of Kirkcudbright, and Sir Robert Gordon of Lochinvar. This area was a favourite haunt of pirates because of Kirkcudbright's comparatively large trade with France and Spain, especially in wines. Captured ships were often brought into the port and their cargoes sold off on the quay.

The steamer *Fullwood*, registered in Preston, leaving Kirkcudbright harbour. The jetty was used when tides were low. After the Battle of Langside, King Philip of Spain fitted out a fleet carrying a large army to avenge the wrongs done to Mary, Queen of Scots, and there is a tale that the place fixed for the Spanish landing was Kirkcudbright. Historical references to the town's harbour are many, and on more than one occasion Kirkcudbright was designated as the best harbour for an invasion fleet to anchor in. Following the Revolutionary Settlement of 1689 there were numerous Jacobite plots to put a Stuart King back on the British throne, and part of King William's fleet carrying the troops for his invasion of Ireland embarked at Kirkcudbright. A prominent building on the Mote Brae was the Basil Warehouse, erected in 1734 'for the purposes of the Baltic Trade'.

The Mote or Moat Brae, first referred to in 1632, is the area bounded by the low wall on the far side of the river. It originally extended much further into the river, and being surrounded by water on all but the landward side formed an important feature of Kirkcudbright's defences during the Middle Ages. A friary, a house of the Friars Minor Conventual (the original branch of the Franciscan Order), once stood on the castle side of the Mote Brae. Following the Reformation the friary buildings passed to Sir Thomas MacLellan of Bombie who sold them to the town council in 1570, with the exception of the former chantry chapel, known as MacLellan's aisle, which he retained as a burial place for his family. The only surviving part of the friary, it is now incorporated into the present Greyfriar's Church, of which it forms the sanctuary. The conventual buildings were demolished and the stone used to build MacLellan's new town house – MacLellan's Castle. In the nineteenth century there was a boat building yard adjacent to the Moathill, as the Brae was also known.

THE HARBOUR, KIRKCUDBRIGHT.

A comparatively recent photograph of the harbour, demonstrating the shift from commerce to pleasure, with a yacht moored where cargo ships and steamers would once have been. At the turn of the century boating on the River Dee was a popular summer pastime. Small vessels were available for hire, and a contemporary account describes the river busy with leisure traffic, with some vessels even having mouth-organ and fiddle music on board. During the French Wars the Kirkcudbright Shipping Company, comprising members of the incorporated trades and private businessmen, fitted out an armed merchantman named *Britannia* to compete in the coastal shipping trade. She was later disarmed and used in the Baltic timber trade and was eventually wrecked. Two of her cannon lay in the Tolbooth for many years and were brought out on festive occasions. In the state papers of King Henry VIII, dated October 1514, it is recorded that 'Rouxel of St Malo, in his vessel *La Pourrye*, captured a Spanish ship before Karcowbray'.

B6782. J.V.

THE HARBOUR, KIRKCUDBRIGHT.

A ship at anchor in the new harbour, *c.*1912. The Dee salmon fisheries were once famous. The fisheries started below Tongland Falls and used to average 1,800 fish per annum up to the 1930s. Salmon were despatched to markets in Liverpool, Manchester and even London. The cargo list for the steamship *Countess of Galloway* on 22 March 1854 includes the entry '1 Fish'. Latterly the numbers of Dee salmon have fallen drastically to under one hundred fish per annum.

223419.JV. OLD KIRKCUDBRIGHT.

The road alongside the Academy, leading to Castledykes. The pensioner's houses of Wheatcroft now stand to the right. MacLellan's Castle, one of Kirkcudbright's most important landmarks, is now a scheduled ancient monument under the care of Historic Scotland. Never designed as a defensive building, it comprises a lot of typical architectural features of the sixteenth century, when such residences were making the transition from grim fortresses to comfortable houses. In the mid-eighteenth century, the roof was removed by Sir Robert Maxwell of Orchardton, who became proprietor of the castle through his marriage into the MacLellan family, and was put onto the mansion-house which he was building at Orchardton, near Auchencairn. The iron stanchions were taken out of the castle windows to make agricultural implements at Orchardton.

Local celebrities taking tea in the Paul Jones Tea-room in St Cuthbert Street. The couple on the right are the noted artists Jessie M. King and E.A. Taylor. Nettie Houston, sitting facing the camera, was art teacher at the Academy. She and her sister used to play the violin at the Academy's annual Candlemas Ball. Jessie M. King was one of the group of artists dubbed the 'Glasgow Girls'. She designed the interior of the tea-room – the John Paul Jones theme was her idea – as a thank-you to the owner, Mr Murdoch, who had been kind enough to extend credit to hard-up members of Kirkcudbright's artists' colony. The waitresses are Mollie Lockhart and Jackie McAdam. Their pirate costumes were also designed by Jessie M. King. Other artists resident in Kirkcudbright included E.A. Hornel, Charles Oppenhemier, William Robson and more recently Tim Jeffs.

GREEN-GATE-CLOSE, KIRKCUDBRIGHT

Greengate Close was purchased by Jessie M. King in 1908. After teaching in Paris, she and her artist husband, E.A. Taylor, came to live permanently in Kirkcudbright, and Greengate became the centre of the town's artistic community in the 1920s and 30s. The Taylors restored the cottages which ran down behind the close and let them out, at modest rents, to other artists. The original green gate was part of the fence in front of the house; this was replaced with a door decorated in the 'Glasgow Style' with small pieces of coloured glass. The house and close were originally painted emerald green and that is how the close got its name.

Right: Shorehouse, in front of Harbour Cottage Gallery, as it used to look. The perches lying up against the wall would probably have been used to mark a safe channel in the estuary; due to shifts in the mudbanks there was a potential danger of fishing boats and other vessels running aground. The building has been extensively altered, although the porch still looks much the same today.

A Cottage by the Sea Kirkcudbright

45

This picture is reproduced from a postcard captioned 'On the road to Paradise, Kirkcudbright'. Paradise was a well-known lover's walk and trysting spot – how many local girls were promised a 'walk on the road to Paradise' by young men in years gone by? Much of the walk has now disappeared, and few people know of its existence nowadays because access is no longer easy. During the eighteenth century the Earl of Selkirk, and his son Lord Daer, were responsible for planting much of the local woodland. They introduced oak, beech, ash, elm, birch, chestnut and sycamore and planted hedges along paths such as this and all the roads leading into the town. Many of these hedges still survive today. In the 1791 *Statistical Account*, Robert Muter comments that 'The most charming landscapes will strike the eye, and afford delightful subjects for the poet's fancy, and the painter's pencil'. His prediction has since been proved right!

GOLF CLUB HOUSE, KIRKCUDBRIGHT.

The golf clubhouse used to be at the bottom of Poor House Lane, now Burnside Loaning. In 1911, when the population of the burgh was 2,386, the golf club had a nine-hole course, one-and-a-half miles in circuit and only five minutes walk from the railway station. It was described as being 'well calculated to soothe the mind of the man who has foozled his shot or is badly bunkered'. The club had a ladies branch and the annual subscription was £1, with visitors charged 1/- a day, 3/- per week and £5 per month. The ladies' annual subscription was 10/-.

There were two houses called St Mary's Isle, the first of which was demolished to make way for the second, shown in this photograph. Built in the late 1890's, this thirty-room whinstone mansion was completely gutted by fire in November 1940. A shortage of water hampered the efforts of the firemen and by the time that water from the dam at Cannee Farm had been diverted into a burn, the blaze had taken a good hold. The original building stood on the site of the Priory of Santa Maria de Traill, founded by Fergus, Lord of Galloway, in the reign of King David I. The priory was a large one and the outer gate, called the Great Cross, stood at least half a mile from it. The inner gate leading to the monks' cells was called the Little Cross. The first house is thought to have been built c.1708 from the stones of the priory. Robert Burns visited it when he was entertained by the Earl of Selkirk in 1793. An earlier and much less welcome visitor was the Stewartry seaman John Paul of Kirkbean – better known as John Paul Jones – a captain in the Continental Navy, who raided the house, in 1779, during the American War of Independence, intending to capture the Earl of Selkirk as a hostage to obtain the release of some American prisoners-of-war being held in Britain. Luckily for the Earl he was absent on business, but the raiders carried off some of the family's silver plate. It was returned by Paul Jones several years later with a letter of apology. Tradition has it that Robert Burns first used 'The Selkirk Grace' when he dined at St Mary's Isle with the Earl of Selkirk. He may have composed it beforehand, although most Burns scholars believe that it was delivered impromptu at the dinner party and not prepared in advance.